… OVERCOMING OBSTACLES
& GETTING EXTRAORDINARY
# RESULTS

OVERCOMING OBSTACLES & GETTING EXTRAORDINARY RESULTS

BLAKE LINDSAY

RESULTS FASTER!
PUBLISHING

Overcoming Obstacles & Getting Extraordinary Results
©2022 by Blake Lindsay

All rights reserved. No part of this book may be reproduced or transmitted in any form or by any means, electronic or mechanical, including photocopying, recording or by any information storage and retrieval system, without permission in writing from the copyright owner.

Published by Results Faster! Publishing

Editing by Adept Content Solutions
Cover Design by Debbie Manning Sheppard
Interior Design by Adept Content Solutions

Printed in the United States of America

ISBN: 978-1-7377320-1-3

Contents

Foreword Michael Monteferrante	ix
Chapter One Overcoming Life Obstacles	1
Chapter Two Inspiration for Life Challenges	7
Chapter Three Facing Your Fear	25
Chapter Four Leadership is the Differentiator	31
Chapter Five Building Mutual Trust	43
Photo Gallery	48
Chapter Six Bring Your "A" Game to Break Barriers	67
Chapter Seven Meeting New Challenges with a "Can Do" Spirit	73
Chapter Eight Leap of Faith to New Possibilities	81
Chapter Nine Setting and Reaching Transformational Goals	91
Chapter Ten Commencement: My Compelling Why	99
Personal/Professional Assessment	105
Acknowledgments	112
About the Author	115

Foreword

Michael Monteferrante
President and CEO of Envision

I have had the pleasure of getting to know this extraordinary man, Blake Lindsay, for close to a decade. He is the embodiment of Envision's mission and a terrific spokesperson.

Overcoming Obstacles & Getting Extraordinary Results is entertaining, inspiring, and funny, I'm sure you'll enjoy it as much as I did.

Blake speaking to a large group.

Chapter One

Overcoming Life Obstacles

My life goal, and I believe calling, is to inspire thousands of uniquely challenged people everywhere and help them believe for, expect, and live a fulfilling life. I truly believe it is not where you start, but how you finish that is the measure of your success in life. I am devoted to adding value to people and helping them to finish strong and well. It all starts with connecting with the heart of those you are serving. "People don't care how much you know, until they know how much you care" (Zig Ziglar). Indeed, the more you care, the stronger you are as a leader and a team player.

An inspiring and trusted leader in my life was Zig Ziglar. My father introduced me to Zig when he was serving Positive Life Attitudes for America as a vice-president. Dad arranged for me to go through the very first Born to Win Seminar where Zig was the lead teacher. That was a formative time in my life, and Zig became my friend and mentor. As a result, Zig wrote an endorsement of a book telling my story that I wrote. He wrote:

> *Blind for a Purpose: Turning Life Challenges into Purpose in Life* will open your eyes and your heart in a truly remarkable and encouraging way. Blake Lindsay's writing is forthright, heartfelt and "right on" in every way. As you read what Blake has to say about being blind, I believe you will come to clearly understand that his "vision" is truly remarkable. Chances are good you have your sight, particularly if you are reading the book! But I am excited to be able to say that I honestly believe your vision will be dramatically broadened; your life will be changed and

The more you care, the stronger you are as a leader and a team player.

Teamwork makes the dream work for the discipline it takes to get extraordinary results.

enriched in a wonderful way as you read Blake's story.

Having known Blake and his family for many years, I can tell you they are real—they are solid. This is a production of bedrock America at its best. You will be inspired, encouraged, and undoubtedly find a new lease on your own life in many ways. I believe you will find *Blind for a Purpose* to be well worth the read—and even subsequent re-reads! It's good—really good!

I grew up in a home where faith trumped fear, hope trumped despair, positivity trumped negativity, and high expectations trumped apathy. I learned that a positive heart attitude and a "can do" spirit helps you to do everything more or better. As I have grown older and have been introduced to situations where I can give back, I have acquired an attitude of gratitude. I have moved from an "I can" way of life to an "I'm glad we did" way of being. Teamwork makes the dream work for the discipline it takes to get extraordinary results.

The highway to the top winds upward. The more you accomplish, the farther up you can see. As my dear friend Zig Ziglar would say, I will see you at the top!

> **As you read what Blake has to say about being blind, I believe you will come to clearly understand that his "vision" is truly remarkable.**

My second grade braille teacher Mrs. Davidson, who was one of my first memorable mentors.

Chapter Two

Inspiration for Life Challenges

I have been totally blind since infancy. The cause was a cancerous and potentially life-threatening disease called retinoblastoma. As a result, I have spent most of my life dealing with obstacles and overcoming the challenges that life presents to all of us.

In reflecting upon my life, I have discovered that overcoming obstacles, solving life problems, and finding the right answers to life almost always demonstrates a teacher, coach, or mentor who came along to help us to learn essential life skills or prevail over issues you might not be able to overcome on your own. The best mentors in my life made a world of difference in my success and fulfillment.

One of my favorite true stories from early elementary school at the Indiana School for the Blind resulted in a big victory in my life I have appreciated through the decades. My first momentous learning milestone, taking place in the first grade, was learning Braille. I can still hear the assuring voice of my teacher, Mrs. Palmerlan, as she said, "Blake, let's learn some Braille today." For further encouragement, she told me the story *The Little Engine That Could*, a favorite among children and educators. I recall my brand-new mentor telling me the best and most exciting part of the story, "'I think I can, I think I can,' roared the engine as it successfully made its way up over the high mountains." It was the first time I ever heard this confidence-boosting anecdote, and it certainly convinced me to exert my effort, as I desired to resemble that positive powerful little engine. Somewhere deep inside, I knew that I could too.

Learning Braille was not easy. For the first few months, I was not a fan of Louis Braille, as Braille was difficult to learn and extremely challenging. The letter S resembled the letter P, but with one less dot on the top left. The letter N, felt like O but with one additional dot on the right top side. There are two other sets of letters in the alphabet with similarity.

I was still having difficulty when entering my second-grade year, but my main homeroom teacher, Mrs. Davidson, was a genuine caring encourager who had a true passion for Braille. She took time first to find out specifically which Braille letters were similar enough to frequently fool me. She would then put them side by side so that I could clearly feel and understand the difference between them. Finally, this out of the ordinary code called Braille made sense. Mrs. Davidson was successful in not only helping me to see her vision, but to also make her vision mine. She believed in me before I could believe in myself. That is what great coaches or mentors do. Braille increased my independence, just like she knew it would. It has been a lifetime skill that I dearly cherish.

Dad used to tell us that, "'I Can,' is an attitude, 'I Will,' is an intent, 'I Am,' is taking action, and 'I Am Glad I Did,' or, 'We're Glad We Did,' is nearly always the result." I can review my time and realize many challenges that I met head-on, like this important required challenge of learning Braille. Because of true teamwork, my mentor Mrs. Davidson and I can now proclaim, "We're glad we did."

I am currently the communications and outreach manager with Envision Dallas. We serve those with visual impairment through a variety of employment and education opportunities. Before my current role at Envision, I enjoyed a twenty-two-year career in radio broadcasting as a music personality, which helped me become a well-known voice talent on large and major market radio stations. I now manage my own production company called Blazin' Blake Productions in my spare time.

Prior to joining Envision Dallas, I worked with Zig Ziglar Inspiring True Performance in sales and speaking. It was also my privilege to host the Ziglar Inspire Podcast for several years. Mr. Ziglar was a dear friend and mentor to me. We developed mutual trust and respect, and I learned so much from his mentoring and the many sidebar conversations and coaching moments we shared through the years.

She believed in me before I could believe in myself. That is what great coaches or mentors do.

When we address and overcome our obstacles with effective solutions, we often get extraordinary results.

Previously, I worked at the Bank of America (BOA) and with Dallas Area Rapid Transit. These rich lifework experiences helped me to learn and teach to others the importance of hard work and the significance of having an attitude of gratitude for our family, friendships, education, employment, and life itself.

I am blessed with two optimistic college-educated parents who provided me the opportunity to become a self-directed contributor to society by living for a purpose. Mom and Dad simply wanted me to be the best I could be. They challenged, inspired, and encouraged me and my other siblings to be the best we could be for the world. This good fortune as a child enabled me, a person without sight, to become a role model for those who are living with seeing, hearing, or crippling impairments. Through the years, I have discovered that even people with use of all five senses have their unique challenges. We are all faced with challenges, life issues, and obstacles. When we address and overcome our obstacles with effective solutions, we often get extraordinary results. We are literally turning obstacles into opportunities in every area of our lives, especially the workplace. I take great delight in inspiring and adding value to blind and visually impaired employees and clients of Envision Dallas. It is energizing to help people feel a sense of appreciation as they contribute to the mission and success of the organization and the people we serve.

Each time I apply for a new job, I encounter some apprehension. Most people who interview me have never experienced just how much visually impaired people are able to achieve with today's access technology. Prior to an interview, I usually choose not to mention my blindness. I have the confidence and believe that once we meet and they have gotten over the brief shock of their applicant having no sight, I am completely prepared to eliminate their concerns by presenting my thoughtful responses to their questions and comments. It is essential to answer potential employers' questions honestly and convincingly. When we can present sincere answers and real solutions to their concerns on whether we can fulfill the job responsibilities, it puts the interviewer at ease, and they will nearly always respect who you are and the value you have convinced them you can bring to the job.

In the early 1990s, our independence was on the increase as technology began enhancing the capabilities of people with various impairments. Education and employment have become more feasible than ever before—especially when we put forth our best attitude, extra-mile effort, and a determination to bring value to the department or company. In 1994, I enjoyed an interview with Bank of America (BOA). I properly informed the team exactly what technology and coaching would be necessary for me to succeed as well as someone with no visual impairment would. I knew this profession could be possible if I had a special display known as a Power Braille. I requested Job Access with Speech (JAWS) to work in harmony with the display (i.e., screen reader). They listened in fascination and followed through with my recommendations. The managers were both fascinated and thrilled to learn about these solutions, which enabled me to quickly perform as well as my sighted counterparts. It is necessary to always connect with people who share your challenges and can relate to the top technology for your specific need. The leadership of an organization

It is energizing to help people feel a sense of appreciation as they contribute to the mission and success of the organization and the people we serve.

usually follows through with the best training on behalf of their top performers. I secured the job because of my motivation, determination, and confidence from past successes. But even more importantly, I was able to present effective solutions.

The Bank of America experience was a learning breakthrough. Once I had convinced them I could do the job, I had to study harder than any time in my life to learn policy, protocol, content, and the skills to serve our clients. Furthermore, I learned by listening to leaders who asked the right questions to get the correct answers. Listening became a primary learning skill for me. I also learned to respect my supervisors because they were leaders I could trust. My takeaway was that the best leaders are trustworthy, and that is the key to their influence.

Let me take a moment to summarize some of the technology and tools that is available to blind and visually impaired people today. I previously mentioned Power Braille (i.e., braille display reader), Job Access with Speech (JAWS), Aira sighted glasses, and the many uses of the iPhone, even for navigation. Today's technology provides the blind and visually impaired the tools for significantly greater independence and employability today than any time in my life.

I received promotions each of my seven years of employment with Bank of America. While some people go to work for so much an hour or annual salary, I believe it is essential to consistently do my best work in running with the vision and helping accomplish the mission of the company. Bringing my "A" game to life's challenges, as well as the goals of the workplace, has always been important for me. Through the Bank of America position, I was able to inspire hundreds of workers to do their best work. I have often heard people say with a smile on their voice, "Blake's doing it well. He sets the standard as an overcomer." Our unique impairments can be our best gift to others when we succeed. Hard work and having a positive attitude can truly be inspirational to others in the work force. I strive to be the model of being positive in the workplace. How are you modeling the way?

To function without one of the five senses is difficult for the average person to comprehend until they observe or learn of our joy in becoming 'handy-capable.' Technology will continue to improve in our favor, so please be encouraged. I hope we become even better in convincing employers to take an assessment of our potential productivity, using accessibility tools that help people with blindness or hearing impairments. In most cases employers are relieved and inspired by our confidence and knowledge. It is also important to only apply for employment that you believe you are truly capable of accomplishing with your special skills.

When I was sixteen and tuning out much of what I should have been tuning in, dad introduced me to a person who became my main mentor. I learned that "when the individual is ready, the mentor will appear." That was so true with Zig Ziglar. He was a person uniquely gifted with the style of communication I resonated with and paid attention to. His booming voice and positive expressions accentuated the main points of his message. Zig taught me to turn lemons into lemonade. He encouraged me to focus on who and what was important now and to put my talents into action for the benefit of people. I quickly learned to be solution minded in dealing with objections and obstacles. He also taught me the value of asking the right questions and then helping clients to make the right decision. I quickly learned that we could help people to realize that there is enormous potential in being positive and solution minded even in negative circumstances. What is the lesson we learn from overcoming big obstacles or tests? Go getters and go givers turn tests into testimonies, turn lemons into lemonade, and turn messes into messages.

My parents had educated me on many of Zig's principles beforehand. But when you have not developed into a mature person, it often takes another special someone to reinforce those life lessons learned earlier. Zig was that person for me. People have often commented to me about my optimism and "go get 'em" attitude. I am certain this stems from my loving parents and Mr. Ziglar. As a result, I bring a positive attitude with the passion to inspire all I engage with every day in the workplace. I aim to help and add value in any way I can.

I have authored a book titled, *Blind for a Purpose: Turning Life Challenges into Purpose in Life.*

> I strive to be the model of being positive in the workplace.

> Go getters and go givers turn tests into testimonies, turn lemons into lemonade, and turn messes into messages.

The life stories I highlight generate hope, laughter, and awareness of the challenges and successes that people with unique circumstances, such as blindness, hearing impairment, and mental or physical disability many people are challenged with. There is plenty of proof in the world that people with impairments or what many call handicaps have an opportunity to become the best role models and prove they are "handy-capable." Once I am given the chance to prove to an employer my abilities, along with the required adjustments, when necessary, their apprehension soon vanishes. The people who have given me opportunities have earned my respect and admiration because they have added value to my life. This teamwork also encourages my colleagues when they see the successes, accomplishments, and productivity of handy-capable people. It is fulfilling to know that through my positive attitude and best efforts in the workplace, many others have seen the light through my loss of sight. I am glad when I can blaze a trail for others to do as well and better.

My life goal continues to be to inspire thousands of uniquely challenged people everywhere to expect, work toward, and live a fulfilling life. It is not where you start, but how and where you finish that makes the difference. As Mr. Ziglar would say, "You can get everything in life you want if you help enough other people get what they want."

My friend, *what is your unique ability*? I encourage you to find a trustworthy mentor and spend quality time developing your unique ability for the good of your employer, the benefit of those you can influence, and your own sense of fulfillment.

> The best leaders are trustworthy, and that is the key to their influence.

Think About

1. When faced with life challenges and obstacles, do I have the inspiration and fighting determination to overcome them?

2. What life challenges do I really need to address?

3. What am I doing to find the solution or work the opportunity?

4. What seems impossible to do, but if could be done would fundamentally change everything in my life (Joel Barker, Futurist)?

Blake at the Nasher Sculpture Center.

Chapter Three

Facing Your Fear

As a person who is blind, my life has certainly been interesting. I have learned, however, that we all have hurdles to hop over in life, whether it is blindness or something else, and we can learn a lot from one another's life experiences when we are willing to share them. For the sake of educational entertainment, or a word I like, *edutainment,* I hope we are all taking time to share our significant stories with one another. To get the ball rolling, here is one of my own.

One summer when I was seven years old, my family traveled to Louisville, Kentucky, for a five-day vacation. My parents got me all excited reading the brochure of where we were vacationing and about a high diving board that jutted over the pool. As soon as we arrived, I grabbed my towel and swimsuit and headed to the pool with my family. I will never forget climbing the ladder, counting each step until I reached the diving board. I centered myself by carefully walking down the board until the tips of my toes were touching the end. Standing twelve feet above the water and completely fearless, I leaped into the air. My body tingled as I experienced the free-falling sensation. And then, *SPLASH!*

What a rush! With great excitement, I made that fearless jump more than a dozen times. Little did I know, my high diving fun was about to come to an end.

The adults and kids that were watching me began to tell me how brave I was for jumping at such a dangerous height. Many said they would never do what I was doing and that if I could see how high I was on that diving board, that I would not either. They were sowing fear into my life. They thought they were complimenting me, but as I heard how daring it was, doubt and fear completely consumed me.

So, as I began the much slower climb up the high dive ladder for another flight from the diving board, I became utterly cautious, carefully counting each step up the ladder, which now seemed as tall as Mount Everest. When I finally reached the top, I started to panic as the words of the spectators replayed in my head. I crept for-

> **With great excitement, I made that fearless jump more than a dozen times.**

ward on the diving board at a snail's pace. When my toes felt the end where I had so excitedly leaped off before, terror seized me, and I froze on the edge of the board, teetering over the water.

Dad told me not to be afraid and that it was not an option for me to back down now. He wanted me to face my fear and stand it down, but I was scared. Dad could be kind, but also firm. He commanded me to face this fear since

I had done it so many times before. He was simply trying to teach me the power of negative words and how they can cause us to miss some exciting episodes of our lives if we allow them to take root. Dad knew that I could make the jump at least one more time. He also knew "God does not give us a spirit of fear, but of power, love, and a sound mind" (2 Timothy 1:7).

With eyes wide open, I finally made the jump. *SPLASH!* I came out of the water, grinning from ear to ear. I had conquered my fear for good. I climbed up again and jumped a second time, just for good measure.

That day, I learned a valuable lesson on the high dive. If we are not careful, we can allow people to infuse fear in us even when there is nothing to be afraid of. I appreciate the fact that Dad did not want me to become the victim of unnecessary fear and doubt, but instead to be confident and face challenges head-on.

Perhaps you are facing a high-dive situation in your own life. Do not let fear and doubt hold you back. Today is the day to make a splash. Face your fear. It is often *f*alse *e*vidence *a*ppearing *r*eal.

Think About

1. To what extent do I face my doubts and fear in dealing with surmounting obstacles and challenging work assignments?

2. What fear am I facing now?

3. Fear is often "false evidence appearing real." How can I address this situation from a solution-minded perspective?

4. What must I do to prevail over this issue?

Jennifer, Blake, Congressman Pete Sessions, and David Stupay.

Chapter Four

Leadership is the Differentiator

I grew up in a Christian home. Love was the operative. My mother had earned a Masters in Elementary Education and my father had earned a Doctor of Educational Leadership. My mother Gail, we call her Momma Gail, taught for a few years, and then became a "domestic engineer." She was and continues to be loving and nurturing for the entire family. She does her loving and giving while she is living so she is knowing where it is going. Thanks Momma Gail!

Both parents loved to work and worked their love. They found joy from doing their best work consistently well. They modeled simple acts of faithful stewardship of their love, time, talents, and treasure. I grew up in a real-life proving ground. I learned that the quality of a person's life was in direct proportion to their commitment to their faith and what they believed.

During my childhood I was determined to be independent, self-sufficient, and run with the radio DJ dream in my heart. Sometimes that self-determination and rugged individualism led to the good, bad, and ugly. As John Maxwell would say, "I learned by failing forward."

In my youth and transition to adulthood, I began to learn a major lesson. You learn a lot by listening. Listening is an act of learning. Listening is an act of leading. Listening is an act of connecting with the heart and will of the individual you are communicating with. As a DJ and radio personality, I began to really sharpen my listening skills. However, when I worked in customer service at Bank of America, I really learned to listen to the content and emotion of the message. Many customers were upset, confused, and fearful when they called. I had to understand the issue and be sensitive to the emotion of the customer so I could respond to the issue while dealing with the emotion. I learned to lead the service call by listening.

Another big lesson I learned early in my career was to listen to the advice, teaching, and even correction of wise and trustworthy mentors. I began to really learn that my mother was a wise counselor, and my dad was a good mentor and coach. Furthermore, I learned to listen, really listen, to my supervisors and company leaders. In the process, I grew in understanding and wisdom that led to better performance and a keener sense of fulfillment in my work. I learned what they expected and valued from my work performance in the organization. Best performance is usually a result of high intention, best effort, informed decisions, and skillful execution. When you bring your "A" game to work every day, more good things happen, and a sense of fulfillment follows.

Leadership is the differentiator in creating a winning organization. Leaders make a difference whether the organization is toxic or healthy, low performing or high performing, unproductive or productive, a losing organization or a winning organization giving back to the community. Winning, high-performing organizations are led by passionate, visionary leaders who inspire and energize people to want to accomplish the mission and results that make a difference to employees, customers, and the community as well. Every leader should make the commitment to champion the vision and mission of the organization and model the way for other leadership team members and employees.

You can find about what you want to look for in the workplace. You can find the good, bad, wonderful, and ugly things in the workplace. You can find negativity and dissatisfaction or positivity and satisfaction, mediocrity or top performance, those that add to the culture and those that take away, and those that work for $22 per hour or those who are working to accomplish the mission of the company. I have learned to look for the good, to dig for the gold, and to contribute to the culture and performance of the company.

In my decade of work at Dallas Lighthouse for the Blind and now Envision Dallas, I have worked with three different managerial leadership teams. I have grown to really appreciate and resonate with the current management. I have learned that we must understand, believe in, and share the mission of the organization where we are working. The Envision mission is to improve the quality of life and provide inspiration and opportunity for people who are blind or visually impaired through employment, outreach, rehabilitation, education, and research. I like that. The mission becomes job one for me and fellow employees. I am very proud to say that I have a hand in helping blind and visually impaired people find gainful employment. It is a blessing to get them into a position, to inspire them, and tell their stories of being able to contribute to the success of Envision Dallas and find joy in doing their best work.

Effective leaders understand that quality leadership committed to building a healthy and productive culture is essential in today's high stakes and competitive business arena. The leadership team must recognize that creative thought precedes outstanding performance and productivity. That enables us to deliver quality products and services.

Every leader should make the commitment to champion the vision and mission of the organization and model the way for other leadership team members and employees.

Key phrases in our mission statement that I focus on in working with employees are to "improve the quality of life and provide inspiration and opportunity," and an important part of my work is "creating inspiration in the workplace." Let me share an Envision Dallas story of creating an inviting and inspiring workplace. Ed and Keela Alonzo joined the Envision Dallas team in October 2021. They learned about Envision through their friend John Conly, a gentleman who is totally blind, happily working on our team for over twenty years. Ed and Keela are also totally blind. Envision was especially helpful to the Alonzos by paying for their big move from the small-town Rainelle, West Virginia, to Dallas, Texas. "We weren't getting anywhere where we were living and realized we needed a change," Ed said. "No Uber, Instacart, and most important work opportunities," Keela exclaimed. Ed was born and raised in Amarillo, Texas, for several years. He mentioned it was like moving back to his home state.

This happy couple have been married for around three years and have a stimulating story. "My first husband and Ed's first wife had both passed away. "We were kind of grieving and got on a Blind Singles and Friends group on Facebook where we met and became friends," Keela shared. Ed and Keela are parents of three kids ranging from fifteen to twenty-one years old.

Keela works in sewing on the eTool team, making collapsible shovel bags for the military. Ed manufactures eyeglass cases for our Air Force. "We get up early every day and go to work to make a living, which is the example we show our three kids," Ed detailed. All of us at Envision Dallas, who have gotten the pleasure of knowing Ed and Keela, are inspired by their great work, positive attitudes, and commitment to parenting.

I have learned the following behaviors help people to get talents into action for the benefit of Envision Dallas and their own sense of joy on the job.

1. Bring a positive attitude. A good cup of coffee before leaving home for work is a great way to fire up a positive attitude. Life is a process of leaving and entering. The way I leave home for work affects the way I ar-

rive at work. The way I leave a meeting or complete a call affects how I move into the next activity. Positivity helps you to do everything better.

2. Model the way. Do what you can to set an example by being enthusiastic, prepared, attentive, and on task.

3. Service to others. The best way to be effective is to give yourself in service to others. Outstanding service to and by employees leads a company from good to great.

4. Inspire best relationships and better workmanship. I try to encourage, inspire, and add value to our employees on a day-to-day basis.

5. Help your colleagues. Be ready and willing to help others find answers to their questions, solutions to their problems, decisions for their choices, and resources to get the job done safely and productively.

Not every aspect of our work brings joy on the job. Much of our work can be drudgery unless we are positive and seek to be cheerful. We are at our best when we add enthusiasm at doing good work consistently well. If I can help to cheer the management team or my fellow employees as I work throughout the day, then my labor of love will not have been in vain. The challenge is for all employees to be the best they can be in a healthy and productive culture. To me, finishing well is to leave a legacy of inspiration, help, and service to our employees, donors, and customers. What is your plan to create inspiration in the workplace and help people find joy and fulfillment in their work? Join me in taking a positive attitude to work each day and looking for ways to inspire our co-workers and helping them to make more good things happen for the organization and their own sense of fulfillment.

Think About

1. How well do I inspire others to promote organizational success and outstanding performance in their work?

2. Do I treat others as VIPs and look for sincere ways to encourage, compliment, appreciate, and recognize them for who they are?

3. People will choose us as leaders of influence because they can trust us as servants. What should I do differently or more as a leader of those within my circle of influence?

Blake and Larry on bikes for chapter on trust

Chapter Five

Building Mutual Trust

Trust! I wish what I knew then what I know now. It took me a while to really learn to trust in mentors and coaches. I have come to believe that leadership is both a moral and a spiritual issue. Leadership is an issue of the heart. At the center of the issue is trust. Leadership is built on trust—trusting and being trusted. Trust is modeled and built by leaders serving as mentors or coaches of those in their sphere of influence. Trusted leaders are humble, sincere, and selfless.

I have benefitted greatly by being mentored and coached by leaders I learned I could trust. As a result, I have chosen to become a trusted leader who encourages, inspires, and adds value to those seeking to know, be, and do more in service to many.

Being a trusted leader is a process of loving and treating everyone "as if" they are VIPs. When trust is built, then the trusted leader of influence can help to pull out the best in everyone. The leadership modeling and mentoring process becomes a way of life, leading to joy and fulfillment in the relationship.

Let me share how I began to learn to trust. In the spring of my second-grade year, dad proudly accommodated my request to remove the training wheels from my bike. I first learned how to ride a bicycle in the front yard with both Mom and Dad walking on each side of me. Once I was confident riding in our front yard, Dad bought a nice, two-seated bike called a tandem from a retired couple right before my ninth birthday so I could learn to ride on the street. The retired couple was pleased that a blind boy and his dad would enjoy the bike while having quality conversations along the way. The bike had three "meters," including a speedometer, tachometer, and an odometer which had only twenty miles registered.

> Leadership is an issue of the heart. At the center of the issue is trust.

> Being a trusted leader is a process of loving and treating everyone "as if" they are VIPs.

A couple of times each week during the summer and early fall, Dad and I rode in tandem on a six-mile journey. The ride took us approximately thirty-six minutes to complete, as we averaged ten miles an hour. Throughout the last couple of minutes of our rides, we traveled at our top speed of twenty-five miles per hour, resembling an eager horse running for the barn after a vigorous day's work.

Dad had been a high school coach and was physically fit, so his legs were much stronger than mine, so when we would speed up to around twenty-eight miles an hour, I took the liberty of enjoying a 'Blake Break' until he slowed down to where I could keep up again. It was especially exciting when there was an occasion to try to peddle as fast as a car that would be driving slowly along a residential street. I always hoped the driver saw our speedy team effort.

The next spring, a few months before my tenth birthday, Dad surprised me by putting my hand on the single bike which I often rode in our yard and asked if I would like to follow him on a residential street. I was reluctant but decided to give this a try. I got right behind him and heard him peddling. When he was peddling, he would talk to me so I could stay lined up with him. Initially, I encountered a few accidents but became better and more confident with each ride. I really felt the joy of accomplishment and the importance of trust building.

I quickly learned to stay in Dad's direct path to avoid an unpleasant *ouch* from running into a mailbox, street sign, or curb. I had complete faith my dad would alert me to anything unknown, which could pose a problem. He trusted I would follow his navigational lead from his voice and the noise of his bike. If Dad happened to run over a small object, like a paper cup that had been tossed on the street, I had gotten so good at steering his exact pathway that my two wheels would roll right over the same piece of litter. I was now more at ease than ever and gained great assurance, knowing Dad was leading the way a few feet ahead of me. True victory came when we were able to travel around town with me on my own bike.

It was especially exciting when someone occasionally assumed I was my sighted older sibling Brad, riding along with Dad. They would say, "Hi Brad." I would turn to them with a big happy grin, and say, "Hi, I'm Blake." Since they knew I had no sight, I imagine they thought that was a genuine father-and-son adventure.

Dad lives in Indiana, so we have not lived close enough to consistently ride together for some time. After our more than twenty-year hiatus, and a vacation trip to Indiana, Dad surprisingly suggested that we take this challenging bike ride again. I was a little off the beaten path at first, but within a few short minutes, I was enjoying an incredibly fun time like before. Since I was not as limber as I was twenty years prior, I was relieved to have no accident to report.

During one ride, a friendly neighbor and Sunday school teacher, Dorotha Mack, was riding her bicycle and saw me following Dad in complete trust. I had never met her before, and she turned to me and said with total interest and passion, "Wow! You are doing great!"

A couple of weeks later during a telephone visit with my mother, Dorotha eagerly mentioned that it was very uplifting to her as she was going through a down time. I was thrilled to hear Dorotha was inspired by our demonstra-

My parents, married over 61 years. This was a recent vacation together.

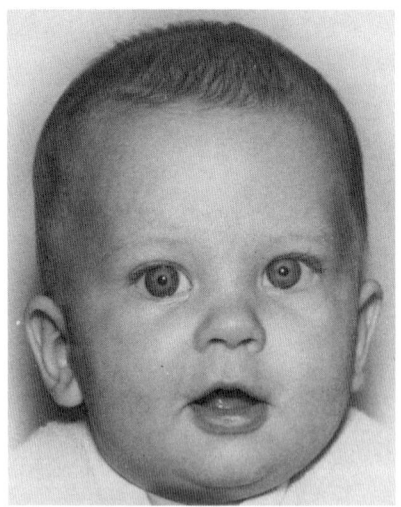

Blake as a baby before his loss of sight.

Blake in the pool, one of his favorite things to do.

Wedding Day, March 29, 2003

An intern at Nasher Sculpture Center taking Blake through the garden.

Blake and friends on White Cane Day.

Blake as the Master of Ceremony at a film festival.

Blake at the microphone and David Stupay looking on.

Blake teaching Braille to young students.

Blake, Congressman Collin Allred, and Jennifer on Capitol Hill.

Blake and Congressman Pete Sessions.

Blake and Senator Ted Cruz.

tion of trust, and that it had reinforced how we should respond to our Heavenly Father.

Most people, myself included, would think that my dad should have been satisfied with us riding together in our stress-free comfort zone on the tandem bicycle; however, when I heard Dorotha's awesome observation, it became obvious to me that God had simply looked ahead and knew that we had some inspiring to do.

Crash right or left! This is another story of building mutual trust and respect in a mentor or coach. My favorite boy scouting memories surround snow skiing trips to Merrimack, Wisconsin. Two winters in a row, we traveled to Devil's Head Resort for three days of unforgettable snow skiing and winter vacation adventures. The snow skiing instructors were specially trained to teach blind people how to ski. I realize now, more than ever, how exceptional these instructors were. Their desire was to leave a thrilling memory for countless people who were blind. They were enthusiastic and confident as they took on this life-sized responsibility. They truly had a special gift for instilling their assurance in us, allowing us to boldly zip down huge hills

> The leadership modeling and mentoring process becomes a way of life, leading to joy and fulfillment in the relationship.

> I really felt the joy of accomplishment and the importance of trust building.

covered in soft white blankets of snow. Our instructors would stay five or so yards behind us as we skied down the hills so they could effectively shout orders to turn right or left in plenty of required time. We also learned the importance of crashing right or left upon demand, which simply means to fall at once to the right or left. Crashing was the quickest and easiest way to stop to avoid an accident. I only had one close call involving a potential collision with another skier who probably didn't know I was blind. Needless to say, I sure didn't see the skier. No calamity occurred because I listened attentively to the commands of my alert instructor—my trustworthy coach. Thank goodness I knew that he was a leader who I could believe in for superior safety.

On many occasions, I have been asked to speak to groups of people specifically on the theme of top performance leadership. I'm delighted to have my own significant example to share with you because it completely illustrates competent, caring, difference-making leadership at its very best. Without my superb ski instructor who demonstrated such leadership, I absolutely could not have made this exhilarating snow skiing memory.

A life lesson learned is how valuable teachers, coaches, and leaders are to our personal and professional development. It is a thrill today for me to be able to give back to others by being a teacher, coach, or mentor in sharing my know-how with others. It is both an honor and a duty for us to share knowledge, skills, and life insights with those seeking our coaching, mentoring, or counsel.

Just like my skiing experience, dad demonstrated the huge impact one person can have on another who is willing to listen, believe, and obey wise guidance and coaching. This is also the kind of trust we should have in our Lord, so that we can enjoy the best quality of life and the most productive results. That said, the big lesson learned is that leaders are always following and leading. We are not all CEOs or head coaches, but we learn to lead by following those we should imitate and learn from. In turn we are better prepared to lead those within our circle of influence.

Think About

1. Who are the mentors or coaches in my life that I have trusted? What issues or obstacles am I currently dealing with where I need a trustworthy mentor or coach?

2. How open, eager, and willing am I to listen, learn, and take action to overcome obstacles or pursue opportunities my mentor is helping me with?

3. You can always accomplish more than you have because you can always become more than you are. What more should I do to make things better for those in my circle of influence?

Blake with Dallas mayor Eric Johnson.

Chapter Six

Bring Your "A" Game to Break Barriers

Convincing employers to look at how much people with blindness are capable of accomplishing is still an obstacle, but much less so with the aid of today's remarkable technology. Each time I get a new job, I meet the same apprehension that people with sight have about working with someone sightless. Unfortunately, many people do not give those who are blind adequate opportunities in the workplace simply because most people have never had the chance to learn about today's useful technology and how much more we are able to achieve with it.

Once I am given the chance to prove to an employer my abilities, along with the required modifications, when necessary, their apprehension completely vanishes. The people who have given me opportunities have earned my respect and admiration because they have added value to my life. It also encourages teamwork when my colleagues see my accomplishments and productivity. I am confident that I add value to any company I work with and that I serve its customers well. It is fulfilling to know that through my positive attitude and best efforts in the workplace, God has enabled many to see the opportunity of employment through my loss of sight.

At age nineteen, I was pleased to have an opportunity to help blaze the trail for my well-deserving, hard-working friend Stephen Kerr. He is blind like me and wanted to get into commercial radio. One summer, when I was nineteen years old, I got to work with K-98 and received positive press on a televised news segment, which reduced thousands of peoples' apprehension by helping them to understand that radio was an excellent and feasible career for blind communicators.

Stephen has a great attitude, and he had the bonus of working with caring people at the station, who helped him excel. Darrel Heckendorf was an engineer determined to take on the challenge of modernizing a blind-friendly radio control room for my friend's employment and independence. For more than twenty years Stephen worked at Entercom's radio KKMJ-MAGIC-95.5 in Austin, Texas. Several years ago, I had the pleasure of meeting with Stephen and Darrel to sample Darrel's creation for myself. His solution to our challenge was simple and completely obliging to me as well. Darrel had laid a full-sized piece of Plexiglas over the computer touch screen and cut finger-sized holes precisely where the functionality was located. A blind person can easily familiarize themselves with the screen by memorizing the exact count to the correct hole in the Plexiglas to execute the specific task needed. Yes! No more Braille labels that easily fall off!

For further convenience, this template folds up and out of the way for those who do not call for this modification. It is a cheap and simple solution to aid those visually challenged in radio broadcasting. It even cuts the need for an assistant, which I had to employ throughout my twenty-two-year radio career. I look forward to using this adaptation some day in my own radio setup.

I often sit and think about the people like Darrel who make such great contributions for the advancement of others. What would life be like without those caring people who focus their inventions on helping others who face unique challenges and disabilities? I thank God for ordinary people who do extraordinary things that make work easier and more productive. I wish an extra special blessing upon Darrel Heckendorf and those creative people who make life better.

Think About

1. How well do I bring my "A" game to accomplish the mission of the organization where I work?

2. How well do I serve as a champion and help the best get better by linking performance goals to company results and doing consistently better-than-good work? Inspired execution is the link between intention and results.

3. To what extent am I enthusiastic and passionate about what is expected of me in achieving company results?

Blake at age 16 with mentor Zig Ziglar.

Chapter Seven

Meeting New Challenges with a "Can Do" Spirit

During my Florida vacation several years ago, I had the opportunity to bond with my then-fourteen-year-old cousin Rhett. Throughout my retreat, I particularly enjoyed hearing Rhett discuss his aspiration to become a chiropractor. Even though I was delighted with his career goal, I enjoyed kidding with him about all the fun he would miss by not choosing a splendid line of work like being a radio DJ. Even though radio had been a decent career for me, Rhett's mother Joy knew that there was a lot more security in his professional preference than mine, so she kindly took me aside and asked me to cease my verbal nonsense. I knew she was right on, so I stopped the teasing. Even though our career choices had no commonality, I really got a kick out of discovering this coincidence: just like my fourteen-year-old cousin, I had set my career goal at the same age. My dream began when I was nine; however, my adolescent voice would not catch up to my vision for another five years.

This visit to Florida has another amusing memory for me. My occasion to bond with Rhett happened to be right in the middle of his baseball season. Rhett's mother handled finding volunteers to perform a variety of duties at the games, and she asked me if I would be the booth announcer for a live game. Rhett echoed his mom, expressing the same request. He figured it would be simple for me to wolf on the mic at the game since I had been a radio DJ for eighteen years. Fresh challenges are exciting for me, and this assignment absolutely fit the bill for two reasons: I know very little about baseball, and I am totally blind. Best of all, it gave me

Meeting New Challenges with a "Can Do" Spirit 75

an opportunity to use my unique broadcasting ability in a new way.

Now, it is not as dumb of an idea as you would think. Uncle Marvin ran the scoreboard beside me, and he has a vast knowledge of baseball and the jargon to go along with the sport. With this winning combination and team effort, he could communicate to me what I needed to convey to the crowd. Uncle Marvin and I embraced our brand-new challenge and willingly accepted our mission.

As blessing would have it, my mom and I were together on this trip. She sat in the booth with us, along with her two sisters, which really made this event an extra-special occasion for all of us.

With Marvin's expert help, I confidently announced all the player's names with enthusiasm. We got into a rapid rhythm with Marvin passing on to me what to say after each play. His voice did not come through the speakers because of my quick finger operating the microphone's on and off switch. I had a blast being the guest announcer known as Baseball Blake for the duration of the game. Through Uncle Marvin's eyes, along with his assortment of baseball lingo and great sense of humor, I was able to boom out all kinds of brand-new baseball terminology throughout the afternoon. The spectators had no clue that there was a blind dude in the booth behind that mic. But the most satisfying part to me was that my limited knowledge on baseball did not deter my delivery at all.

I believe that the pleasure I got from doing that live event resembled the buzz actors and actresses get when they perform as an authority on a subject that they, in many instances, are not especially knowledgeable on. How do you face obstacles or challenges that are limiting your results?

First, be determined to meet the challenge. You can do it! Remember, as Joe Sabah says, "You don't have to be great to start, but you have to start to be great!"

Second, you need to have a team environment. Decide who to collaborate with and who will help you to see your challenge more clearly. I would not have been successful without my caring uncle Marvin by my side as my necessary "seeing eye person."

Meeting New Challenges with a "Can Do" Spirit 77

Third, when faced with a challenge—dive in! I love the saying, "Anything worth doing is worth doing imperfectly until you can learn to do it perfectly." We all need to seize the opportunity to use our unique ability as often as we can. Do it and grow in the process.

Finally, think about what worked well and how you felt about it. As you reflect on successful events, you can begin to use those positive feelings as an anchor and draw upon them when faced with future challenges.

I do not know that I will ever call another baseball game, but I am up for the challenge! Are you up for the challenges facing you? Rhett certainly was. He is now a licensed chiropractor and fitness coach in Florida.

Marvin challenged me to do something I had never done before that expanded my capacity. He served as a mentor and team player in setting the tone and feeding me with the information to broadcast the game. That is so true in the workplace where every day, we are seeking a better way to stay abreast of the knowledge, skills, and tools it takes to compete in the marketplace. A high-performing and productive organization can achieve the intended results if the leader's heart is focused on helping even the best to get better—to expand their capacity. The inspirational and forward-looking leader sets the tone for a dialogue of renewal and continuous improvement. As a leader are you bringing your "A" game in building a healthy high-performing culture. Be a contender! Much of our work and meeting new challenges can be drudgery unless we are positive and seek to be cheerful in the workplace. We are at our best when we add enthusiasm and a "can do" spirit to doing everything consistently well.

Think About

1. What new learning or leadership challenge do I need to pursue?

2. To what extent can open and honest communication influence how well the organization or department will function in pursuing the intended results?

3. In what ways am I bringing energy and passion to help employees get their talents into action for the good of the organization or department and their own sense of fulfillment?

4. Where can I expand my capacity in making more good things happen in my life and with my workplace colleagues?

Blake and his exciting skydive experience.

Chapter Eight

Leap of Faith to New Possibilities

My lifetime of total blindness constantly offers me opportunities to challenge and inspire people of all ages to set significant goals and to follow through with a personal development plan. My dad taught me to seize the opportunity life present to you. He often said, "As good as we are, how can we get better?"

For several years, I had the privilege of speaking with a bright group of high school seniors who were together for a three-day business program called Camp Enterprise. I will never forget the time I was finishing my talk in a segment I call "Ask the Blind Guy." This is my audience's opportunity to indulge their curiosity with questions about the daily experiences of a person without sight. I can usually encourage people to be comfortable in asking what they want to know. During this occasion, I was asked something which I had never been asked before. "Blake, is there anything you haven't done on your list of adventures that you want to experience? I blurted out the first response that came to mind. Skydiving! I told them that going skydiving had fascinated me for many years. However, in reflecting upon the question on my commute home, I could not remember ever wanting to skydive.

Two weeks later, I received a surprise call from Charles with the Rotary Club of Dallas. Charles said, "We are sponsoring you on a skydive, so when can you go?" My first thought was, *Wow! Did I really say I wanted to skydive*? I at once realized I had, and now it was time for me to follow through with my impulsive response. We set up the best time for the adventure to take place, when I could be accompanied by a willing and qualified instructor.

Surprisingly, I became more excited and less nervous with each passing day. As I thought about this fearful goal of skydiving, I began envisioning how it could help me to inspire people to dive into their goals and face their fears in life.

I was grateful to be able to go in one day before my jump, because it was imperative to have some training on how to position my body and what I should expect. This valuable education came from my instructor, Ernie Long. Frequent sky divers took special interest in my upcoming experience. I enjoyed their eagerness to share knowledge. They could hardly wait to see me encounter what they knew would be a blast for a blind guy—or anyone for that matter. I completed the forms that mentioned death in several places. When I returned home, I called friends and family to state that I expected complete safety, but if something should happen, I wanted them to know how much I cared about our relationship. I knew that if I did have an accident, I was ready to leave this phase of life and be taken to my permanent home. So, I then paid our bills in advance and even showed my wife Jennifer how to take care of them online, using our computer and telephone automation.

I asked my good friends Glen and JD if they would make a video recording of this exciting, but fearful event. They quickly agreed and came along on the adventure.

The day of the leap of faith, Glen and I drove out to a peaceful and beautiful wooded area to record my feelings before this event took place. It was a beautiful Saturday morning without a cloud in the sky. The winds were gently blowing at eight miles per hour. Glen's awesome interview also captured in audio the wonderful sounds of nature and even a distant noise of our public light rail transportation train passing by.

After our extraordinary start to an exciting Saturday, we got into Glen's car and proceeded to arrive at Skydive Dallas. I will never forget how much I enjoyed our one-hour drive and visit up to Whitewright, Texas. Glen and I talked about the meaning of our life that beautiful morning. We arrived ahead of schedule and enjoyed a quick bite for lunch. Glen and I then walked outside to observe all the other people skydiving. Our outside temperature was a warm eighty-eight degrees, which felt just right with the light breeze.

JD soon arrived. *The Dallas Morning News* had graciously agreed to write my story. I got a detailed interview from a pleasant lady with the cool memorable name, Holly Hacker.

Now it was finally time to climb into the plane, with twenty-three tightly fitted sky divers. I was excited to at last be taking that leap of faith I had expected throughout the past two weeks. I would not be in the unknown skydiving zone much longer. I was alert and attentive as we climbed up to 13,500 feet and prepared to jump with my experienced instructor Ernie Long.

Our leap into the sky at 13,500 feet was like no other feeling I have ever felt before. For one, the temperature is thirty degrees cooler at 13,500 feet than it is on the ground. So, what had been a balmy eighty-eight degrees was now an exhilarating fifty-eight in the sky. We hit the air at about 140 miles per hour and kept that momentum as we dropped for sixty seconds. The rapidly changing pressure caused me to temporarily, and a little painfully, lose my hearing. That part did not take away my rush of memory-making excitement. Following one full minute of free-falling, our parachute deployed. I then had an opportunity to carry out hearing retrieval tricks as if I were descending from the sky in a jet for landing. My instructor, Ernie, began performing exhilarating maneuvers, showing me how much control, he had in steering us with the steering strings attached to our parachute. I got a kick out of quickly turning left, then right, followed by moving backwards and forwards. "Wow!" I exclaimed.

When we comfortably and safely landed, all the spectators applauded. This exceptional experience is among my most exciting and most valuable in my lifetime to date. Each time I reflect upon the skydiving experience, it seems I learn another lesson in how to live my life more fully and to inspire others to enjoy the same. I am more determined than ever to motivate people to be the best they can be in finding joy in life at work, at home, and in the community every day.

Glen used his remarkable talent by taking the amazing pictures which he and JD took and produced ten- and five-minute videos showing and telling my unique story. This was a very helpful keepsake production. It helps me encourage people to dive in and face their fears, set transformational goals, and meet obstacles, which inevitably come, head-on.

Another twist to the story occurred five years ago when I lost my good friend Glen from a heart attack. I was concerned I would not enjoy hearing this experience played back on the video that I show when speaking to people about diving into their goals and challenges. Quite the opposite has happened, though, as I smile each time I hear Glen and recall our best bonding time ever. Please make memories with those you love. These thoughts are part of our happiness.

When we dive into our goals and face our obstacles, it can resemble my skydive experience by becoming "faith and fun all in one!"

Here's a link, to the short video of this special experience: http://blakelindsay.com/videos/leap-of-faith/

I learned a lot about life with this experience. I often remind myself we learn a lot by listening. I was especially attentive to the instructions of my mentor and coach. I listened, really listened, before making the leap. My mentor shared the vision and execution instructions for the leap, giving meaning to teamwork. His coaching helped me to face my fears with the assurance that he knew how to execute the jump for a safe landing. Once again, I saw the need for a professional mentor. It gave me confidence to continue to use my expertise to inspire and mentor others. This is simply one more illustration of how teamwork becomes more than one-plus-one.

> **It helps me encourage people to dive in and face their fears, set transformational goals, and meet obstacles, which inevitably come, head-on.**

Think About

1. To what extent am I open to new and exciting possibilities?

2. To what extent am I helping my fellow employees or those I mentor to be open to possibilities?

3. Successful moments flow out of opportunities that challenge and stretch us. In what ways do I have the resolve to take risks in making difficult decisions?

Blake with skydiving instructor.

Chapter Nine

Setting and Reaching Transformational Goals

Through the years, I have purposely become more disciplined in eating right, exercising daily, and working smarter. As a result, I am happier, and I feel a greater sense of accomplishment and contribution in making things better. There is potential in goal setting that can transform your life. Personal development usually leads to better health, greater fulfillment, more happiness, greater contentment, and success in life. Setting and reaching goals in your personal and professional life enables you to do more for yourself and the company as well.

I started doing an annual self-assessment and goal setting when I took my dad's advice that I should get my own annual tune-up. He often challenges me with the question, "As good as we are, how can we get better?" My good friend Zig Ziglar called this a "check-up from the neck-up."

In setting and reaching transformational goals, I started asking myself four important questions on the same day each year and Brailling and typing down my responses. I present this concept to you in hopes that you will receive the same results I have over the past two decades.

1. How am I more knowledgeable today than I was one year ago? Expand this thought by asking yourself, what can I do to increase my knowledge for the current year ahead?

2. How am I more capable today than I was one year ago? This can be learning another language, mastering new technology, developing a new competency, completing a course, or anything that will grow your knowledge and core competencies in a productive manner.

3. How am I more confident today than I was one year ago? Am I currently doing activities and learning about things that matter? Will they make me feel more empowered to help others, along with myself? Will they help me to make more good things happen at home, in the workplace, or in my community?

4. How am I more influential today than I was one year ago? I follow up with what I am doing currently to improve my example so that I can be a better role model who encourages others.

This process has taught me that you measure the size of your accomplishment by the obstacles you must overcome to reach your goals. No matter what your age is, my challenge for you today is to become the person you want to be in the world. You do not have to be the best in the world. Just be the best you can be for the world. I believe that if you engage in the enthusiastic pursuit of the four following goals, you will notice an annual transformation that you will be pleased with. As they say, we can move from

> Setting and reaching goals in your personal and professional life enables you to do more for yourself and the company as well.

> Outstanding service to many leads to greatness in your leadership role.

Setting and Reaching Transformational Goals

good to great. Outstanding service to many leads to greatness in your leadership role. Use the following four questions to set new goals. Goal achievement enables you to do more for your family, workplace, church, and community. What are your dreams? Goals are dreams we put into plans and act on to fulfill!

1. Set a goal and action plan to become more knowledgeable by one year from now.

2. Set a goal and action plan to become more capable by one year from now.

3. Set a goal and action plan to become more confident by one year from now.

4. Set a goal and action plan to become more influential by one year from now.

There is the potential in setting and reaching goals that can transform your life. It does not matter when you begin your mission, so you might as well start today. As Zig Ziglar would say, "It is not where you start but how you finish that makes the difference."

When it comes to organizational or company goals, the focus should be on results. Even the best companies can get better when they focus goals on intended results and execute well. Execution is the key in moving from intent to results. I have observed that high-performing and productive organizations often achieve the intended results when the leader's heart and soul is focused on the culture and mission of the company or department. Inspirational leaders set the tone for the dialogue of continuous improvement, leading to results in an organization. They are fearless to make difficult decisions and solve problems that are obstacles limiting or hindering results. They do not fear negative reactions to the well-informed decisions they make. As a result, they frequently communicate a shared vision that inspires "all-in" employee engagement to increase productivity and surpass the goals of the company.

Think About

1. In what ways do I take appropriate risks in overcoming obstacles to achieve worthwhile goals?

2. If you address the need, you will never lack for a worthwhile goal. What do you need to do better or differently?

3. What teamwork or resources do I need to achieve my goal?

4. As a result of achieving this goal, "I'm going to get better than good at . . . !"

Blake doing radio production.

Chapter Ten

Commencement: My Compelling Why

We have all heard, "Today is the first day of the rest of your life." That is how I am starting this chapter. I do not want this to be a conclusion to your journey in overcoming obstacles and making a difference in your life and that of others. I want it to be a commencement of a journey of knowing, being, and doing more for those in your circle of influence, your family, and yourself.

I have written this book to encourage you to develop and use your unique talent and ability to make things better in every area of your life. I truly believe that a positive heart attitude and a "can do" spirit helps us to do everything more or better. It is a matter of being the best we can be in service to others. How are you doing? As good as you are, how can you get better in making a greater difference? My friend, "Let us consider how we may spur one another on toward love and good deeds" (Hebrews 10:24).

I have spent most of my career in radio, banking service, and outreach for Envision Dallas. It has been my privilege to encourage and see hundreds upon hundreds of people overcome obstacles and be transformed into contributing citizens, finding joy in their work and experiencing fulfillment in the process. A classic example is the story of Joyce Hudson. Joyce is an appointment specialist with Bold Sales Solutions. She appreciates Envision Dallas very much.

Her relationship with Envision Dallas began while she was in high school. Ultimately, Envision Dallas's involvement in her life led to her current customer service position where she contacts Better Business Bureau–accredited businesses to promote advertising options.

Joyce has accomplished so much since her days in the seventh grade when her homeroom teacher observed that she was having difficulty seeing the board clearly. It was affecting not only her class participation but her overall grades. Once contacted by Joyce's teacher, her mother then took her to an eye doctor. The diagnosis was early macular degeneration.

Small magnifiers and a closed-circuit TV (CCTV) were necessary for Joyce to read and write. CCTVs were so large at the time that they were only located in libraries. During high school, Joyce's teachers and principal suggested that she transfer to the Texas School for the Blind and Visually Impaired in Austin. That was not an option for Joyce. "I wanted to remain in a normal class setting," Joyce said.

Her school coordinated with Envision Dallas, then known as Dallas Lighthouse for the Blind, who teamed up with a local Lions Club to create large-print books. "With this help, I graduated a year early," Joyce said with glee in her voice.

She then went to college, graduating with an associates in science degree as well as a bachelor's in social work.

"Throughout college, Envision Dallas supported me with my visual needs," Joyce said.

"They even helped me find a job with the state, working in child protective services." The leadership at Envision Dallas is pleased to have a positive, productive, hard-working person such as Joyce on the team.

Envision Dallas exists to encourage and help blind and visually impaired people to develop and use their unique ability to make things better at home, in the workplace, and in their community.

Living to me means caring for and being responsive to people who come across my path. It means sharing issues and emotions. It means really listening to others and feeling with them. So, be compassionate with each other. Take responsibility for making life and life around us better. As we learn these lessons, we are on a wonderful journey to a better place.

I close with a quote from George Bernard Shaw. "Life is no brief candle to me. It is a sort of splendid torch which I have gotten hold of for the moment, and I want to make it burn as brightly as possible before handing it on to future generations." As an old hymn goes, "If I can help somebody as I travel along, then my living shall not be in vain."

Think About

1. It is my hope that tomorrow, the world will have compassionate forward-looking leaders who can inspire and pull out the talents of those choosing to follow them in building a winning organization. Will I be such a leader of influence?

2. It takes courage to be a leader employees will eagerly choose to follow. What must I do for others to choose me as a leader?

3. Am I engaging and energizing fellow employees to become better and more capable that they otherwise would be?

Overcoming Obstacles and Getting Extraordinary Results

Thinking, Acting, and Influencing Skills

For each of the behaviors noted below, use the following scale to assess your need to improve in that area. "Need to improve" represents the relative gap between your current skill level and how good you *are determined to be*. Circle your score from 1 to 5 with 5 being "no improvement needed."

Great Improvement Needed	Considerable Improvement Needed	Moderate Improvement Needed	A Little Improvement Needed	No Improvement Needed
1	2	3	4	5

1. When faced with life challenges and obstacles do I have the inspiration and a fighting determination to overcome them?

1	2	3	4	5

2. To what extent do I face my doubts and fears in dealing with surmounting obstacles and challenging work assignments?

1	2	3	4	5

3. Am I seeking mentors to help me overcome obstacles by reflecting on my actions and practices, using the learning to inform future decisions and actions?

1	2	3	4	5

4. How well do I inspire others by promoting and celebrating organizational success and outstanding work of fellow employees?

1	2	3	4	5

5. Do I treat my associates as VIPs and provide them a balance of mission motivation with sincere compliments, encouragement, and appreciation?

| 1 | 2 | 3 | 4 | 5 |

6. Am I open and responsive to knowledge or influence from mentors and organizational leaders and the possibilities they offer?

| 1 | 2 | 3 | 4 | 5 |

7. How effective am I at developing and earning trust with leaders and employees?

| 1 | 2 | 3 | 4 | 5 |

8. Do I listen, really listen, to learn with trustworthy leaders and employees when seeking creative solutions or growing professionally?

| 1 | 2 | 3 | 4 | 5 |

9. How well do I champion the organizational mission and a shared vision that is compelling and helps fellow employees to bring their "A" game to the workplace?

| 1 | 2 | 3 | 4 | 5 |

10. Am I learning to lead by asking the right questions in helping others to find their own answers and solve their own problems?

1	2	3	4	5

11. Am I making a positive impact on fellow employees that affects the quality of our collective work?

1	2	3	4	5

12. Do I model and encourage a "can-do" spirit and enthusiasm for continuous improvement in the hearts and minds of fellow employees?

1	2	3	4	5

13. How well can I envision and pursue answers and solutions in new and different ways?

1	2	3	4	5

14. Do I really understand that vision without competence, technique, and execution is blind?

1	2	3	4	5

Overcoming Obstacles and Getting Extraordinary Results 109

15. To what extent do I become well informed and decisive in the face of uncertainty?

| 1 | 2 | 3 | 4 | 5 |

16. Do I do it now with the understanding that hesitation plus procrastination results in a desperation situation?

| 1 | 2 | 3 | 4 | 5 |

17. How well do I find ways to take risks in overcoming obstacles to achieve worthwhile goals?

| 1 | 2 | 3 | 4 | 5 |

18. Can I manage the short-term results now while working toward achieving long-term goals?

| 1 | 2 | 3 | 4 | 5 |

19. How well do I practice the discipline of getting results—extraordinary results?

| 1 | 2 | 3 | 4 | 5 |

20. How effective are we at turning our plan into specific results for growth and productivity?

| 1 | 2 | 3 | 4 | 5 |

Overcoming Obstacles and Getting Extraordinary Results

21. Which are the three skill items that represent the greatest need for improvement for you?

_____

_____

_____

22. Given the assessment, what is the first thing you intend to do differently?

_____

_____

_____

_____

_____

_____

_____

_____

_____

"Are we going to get any better, or is this it?"

Assessment Summary

Inspiring Leadership
If your score was from 95 to 100

A Little Improvement Is Needed
If your score was 90 to 94

Improvement Is Needed
If your score was 85 to 89

Considerable Improvement Is Needed
If your score was 80 to 84

Great Improvement Is Needed
If your score was 79 or below

Acknowledgments

My story has not developed in isolation. I have so many people that have mentored, coached, affirmed, and encouraged me through the years. The stories shared in this book are dedicated to anyone seeking to know, believe, and be the best they can be for the world.

This project would not have been possible without the love and care of my wife, Jennifer. She is always there for me whether meeting with mayors or congressman or traveling to speaking events locally and nationally.

I count my blessings for my loving parents, Dr. Larry and Gail Lindsay. Mother (Momma Gail) and Dad (Grandoctor) have been great mentors to me throughout my life. They have always believed in me and pointed me in the right direction.

I am grateful for my sister Molly and my brothers Brad, Bryce, and Brock. They have loved and helped me to live a normal life as a blind child.

I was blessed to be a friend and member of master motivator Zig Ziglar's team. Zig was a special mentor to me at a transformational time in my life. Zig, his wife Jean, Tom, and the Ziglar family treated me with respect and dignity in making me feel part of the family.

There would be no book without the incredible support and counsel of three key individuals. Tony Jeary, well known as the results guy, has inspired, and directed the writing of this book. He championed a book and speeches aimed at encouraging everyone to overcome obstacles and get extraordinary results. At Envision Dallas, I report directly to David Stupay. He has been a pillar of strength and an effective motivator. David is a super husband to Vanessa Stupay who is the ideal mother and wife. They have three wonderful children. My dad has also been a source of encouragement, wisdom, and editorial help in completion of this project.

As a person who is totally blind, I now "see" things even more clearly through the writing of this book. For my readers, I pray my stories in this book will make you laugh, think deeply, and appreciate the true beauty of life and all that it has to offer. May my stories also bring you hope, joy, and a greater sense of purpose to your lives. It is my hope that through this book you will appreciate having your "Eyes Wide Open" even more today than you did yesterday. "With God all things are possible" (Matt. 19:26).

About the Author

Blake Lindsay has served as the manager of outreach and communications with Envision Dallas for thirteen years. Totally blind since infancy, from retinoblastoma, a cancer condition, Lindsay offers a unique perspective on all aspects of Envisions programs, services, and employment. He is a resident expert on overcoming obstacles and life challenges and has helped thousands to become what he calls handy-capable.

Blake is a well-known voice talent on top Texas, Kansas, and Indiana radio stations. He also manages his own production company Blazin' Blake Productions. He produces nationwide radio and TV branding and commercials and specialized branding for various businesses.

Blake has served as the owner-manager of Blazin' Blake Productions since 2005. He also served as vice president for four years and president for five-plus years of the Marquis at Preston Park Homeowners Association. He has also served as a certified advocate with the National Industries for the Blind for ten years.

Blake has authored two books: *Out of Sight Living: A Sightless Person with Pure Vision*, as well as *Blind for a Purpose, (Turning Life Challenges into Purpose in Life*.

Prior to joining Envision Dallas, Lindsay worked with Zig Ziglar Corporation, Dallas Area Rapid Transit (DART), and Bank of America.

Blake's inspiring message brings a positive life attitude and spirit of encouragement to his life purpose of helping people improve their attitude, perception, and understanding of blindness or other physical and mental life challenges.

Envision the Possibilities

Envision Dallas provides meaningful employment opportunities to the people in the North Texas area who are blind or low vision. We work with people to help build independence in all areas of their lives.

Our programs and services include:

- Low Vision Clinic
- Serving Our Seniors Program
- Assistive Technology Lab
- Orientation and Mobility Training
- Esther's Place Model Apartment

We invite you to see firsthand how the people at Envision Dallas are overcoming obstacles and thriving every day.

Come tour our facility by calling us at 214-420-6411 or email blake.lindsay@envisionus.com.